Praise for *The*

'As a craftsman I found myself savouring the flavours of this delicately wrought book; as a human I commend to you the soul of this little girl, the world's child.' **Bruce Pascoe**

'Exquisite, devastatingly timely ... concise, poetic, poignant and persuasive.' **Poppy Gee**

'Achingly beautiful ... Will the world ever listen to Palestine? ... Read and weep.' **Witi Ihimaera**

'Searing, honest, raw. This stunningly beautiful portrayal of exile and loss both broke and healed my heart at once. I have bought copies for many of my loved ones so they too can find comfort in its pages.' **Tess Woods**

'The delicacy of Sara Haddad's novel is a triumph for literature ... This book is a "must read" of our times. As the great Palestinian American Edward Said would say, "It speaks truth to power."' **Peter Manning**

'Gives aching resonance to the loss and longing, and ultimately the resilience, of the Palestinian people.' *The Sydney Morning Herald*

 Sara Haddad is an editor and writer who has worked in publishing for thirty-five years. A Lebanese Australian, she lives on Gadigal land with her husband and two children. She hopes that one day all Palestinians will be free to return to their country and live there without fear.

For my mother and father

THE SUNBIRD

Sara Haddad

UQP

Originally published in 2024 by Doubledown
Published in 2024 by University of Queensland Press
PO Box 6042, St Lucia, Queensland 4067 Australia
Reprinted 2025 (twice)

The University of Queensland Press (UQP) acknowledges the Traditional
Owners and their custodianship of the lands on which UQP operates. We
pay our respects to their Ancestors and their descendants, who continue
cultural and spiritual connections to Country. We recognise their valuable
contributions to Australian and global society.

uqp.com.au
reception@uqp.com.au

The names on the inside front cover are those of villages that were
depopulated and/or destroyed in the Nakba of 1948.

Cover illustration and design by Tam Morris
Typeset by Graeme Jones
Printed in Australia by McPherson's Printing Group

University of Queensland Press is
assisted by the Australian Government
through Creative Australia, its principal
arts investment and advisory body.

University of Queensland Press is assisted
by the Queensland Government through
Arts Queensland.

A catalogue record for this book is available from the National Library
of Australia.

ISBN 978 0 7022 6920 2 (pbk)
ISBN 978 0 7022 7090 1 (epdf)
ISBN 978 0 7022 7091 8 (epub)

University of Queensland Press uses papers that are natural, renewable and
recyclable products made from wood grown in well-managed forests and other
controlled sources. The logging and manufacturing processes conform to the
environmental regulations of the country of origin.

CONTENTS

AUTHOR'S NOTE

'You write in order to change the world ... If
you alter, even by a millimeter, the way people
look at reality, then you change it.'
James Baldwin

My connection to Palestine began the year I
was born, 1967. Following the Six-Day War,
or *Al Naksa*, during which Israel annexed what
remained of historic Palestine, the extended
family among whom I was raised began their
long involvement with the issue of Palestinian
liberation. From that point on, justice and

support for Palestine were a given in my world. It was the correct position to take.

My family, who had come from Lebanon, a country that has experienced its fair share of Israeli aggression, railed against biased media reporting, censorship, propaganda and the mendacity of the United States in their unquestioning support of Israel. But I soon realised, as I stepped out into the world, that that was not how the vast majority thought. In this parallel universe, Leon Uris's *Exodus* was accepted as historical fact.

I frequently encountered people who were progressive—except when it came to Palestine. Interactions would become awkward, eye contact would be lost and conversations invariably ended with the predictable, 'It's complicated.'

The Sunbird is the product of both the long-term frustration I have felt over people not knowing, understanding or caring about the truth about Palestine, and a direct and urgent response to the genocide that began unfolding before my eyes in October 2023. I wrote it to educate and to raise awareness. I took my solid knowledge of the issue, acquired over many years, and consolidated it with extensive research. *The Sunbird* is a distillation of this research, my long engagement with the issue, and my own family's experiences—of 1940s village life in the Levant and as Levantine Arab migrants to Australia.

Above all, *The Sunbird* is a labour of love. It is necessarily brief, to counter the narrative that the question of Palestine is complicated, to be read in a single sitting, to be accessible to readers of all ages and all reading levels. The language is clear because the language of liberation is inherently simple: honest, transparent, direct.

It is a relatively gentle entrée to an appalling history and one that I hope will lead readers to explore the issue further.

The Sunbird is a little book but within its pages are myriad references that are portals to greater knowledge and deeper understanding. As Palestinians continue to face attempts to eradicate their lives and culture, *The Sunbird* flies, proudly, defiantly. It belongs to the resistance.

وأقول لنفسِي: سَيطلعُ مِن عَتْمَتِي قَمَر

'And I tell myself: a moon will rise
from my darkness'

Mahmoud Darwish

'I do not agree that the dog in a manger has
the final right to the manger even though he
may have lain there for a very long time.
I do not admit that right. I do not admit, for
instance, that a great wrong has been done
to the Red Indians of America or the black
people of Australia. I do not admit that a
wrong has been done to these people by the
fact that a stronger race, a higher-grade race,
a more worldly wise race to put it that way,
has come in and taken their place.'

Winston Churchill, testimony to the
Peel Commission, formerly known as the
Palestine Royal Commission, March 1937

ONE

واحد

Palestine, December 1947

Crouching like a sunbird ready to fly, Nabila Yasmeen peered through the window of the village school. The children had taken their places, in rows four deep, eager for their learning to begin. The teacher readied himself, straightening books and making notes, pacing the limestone floor until the clock told him that it was time to commence.

Nabila had woken that morning, on this first day of winter, to a fire in the cavernous hearth.

Refusing to budge from her place on the floor while all around her scurried and fussed, she stared, transfixed, at the shimmering flames. Eyelids lazy with sleep, she counted the numbers in her head. And counted them again, just to be sure. She was five-and-a-half years old, exactly. She had worked it out, all by herself, with no one's help. And she wanted him to know.

Staring intently at his face, trying hard not to blink, she fixed her gaze on his mouth. She followed the rhythm of his lips as they drew shapes around words she strained to hear. They said she wasn't old enough yet, but if it were up to her, she would be in that room already, *now*, at a desk, where she belonged. Not out here, pecking at crumbs on the window ledge.

On this day and on others, he indulged her audacity. For a while. At first, he would pretend not to see her, but then she would catch it, the hint of a smile as his eyes darted to the window and then back to the book he held in his hands. He would allow her to remain for as long as it took to read the day's notices, sometimes even for the first few minutes of the first lesson, but then he would send her on her way with a stern stare and a single upward nod of the head.

He was the school's only teacher and he taught the children everything they needed to know. He was firm, tolerant, unwavering in his insistence that education was a privilege, an opportunity to be embraced, fully, fervently. He was good-humoured and easy in his manner, but today Nabila noticed something different in him. He seemed distracted, unsure. There was a lightness missing.

He cleared his throat, adjusted the collar around his neck and began to relay the news that had come to him via the radio. But Nabila found it hard to follow what he was saying. He told his class that, on Monday, the United Nations (whatever that was) had passed something called Resolution 181. He talked of partition and special committees. Of welfare and friendly relations among nations. Of mandates and immigration and freedom of worship. But it soon became apparent that the children in the classroom, most of whom were much older than Nabila, had no idea what he was talking about either.

So, he began again and in the simplest of terms he distilled the information for them. He told them that their country would be divided and a new country formed within it. Nabila was still confused. How could a new country be put inside a country that was already there? Where would the new country go? Where did it come from? What would happen to the people who were already there? Would they be squashed into the ground like ants under a boot? Would Nabila's village be in the new country? Why was this happening? Nabila didn't understand *at all*.

Then came the teacher's cue. Nabila spun on the balls of her agile feet and fled, flapping her arms as she ran to the fields where her mother and father were tending to their land now that the olive harvest was over. Chastened, because she knew she shouldn't have been anywhere near the school, she told her parents what the teacher had said. For a few moments they looked at one another, and then, as they inevitably did with their youngest and most troublesome child, shooed her away with a flick of the hand.

TWO

إثنان

Australia, December 2023

Spring had delivered a heat that made the flies come early. House flies and bush flies and march flies too, flies that swarmed in the air and landed on backs and followed people through front doors so that houses were mad with them. The same heat that had brought the flies had persuaded the jasmine to flower in July and the purple jacaranda to bloom three weeks too soon. Not last summer but two summers before that, the fires had raged and made breathing hard. And then the rain had fallen with such intention that the rivers swelled with dead things and despair.

It's going to be hot today, said Nabila Yasmeen to herself, her small head resting comfortably on the pillow she'd slept on for many years. Between the thumb and forefinger of her left hand she moved the plump corner of her flannelette pillowcase this way and that and watched as the strip below the half-closed blind lightened gradually to reveal the shapes and colours of the world that was coming into focus outside her room. She listened for the koel's call, its rhythmic *whoop* a testament to long days and warm nights. She hadn't always been aware of it, this storm bird, this devil bird, this cuckoo from far away. She was sure it hadn't been here when she'd arrived all those years ago. Still, it wouldn't stay for long. Six months at most. And then it would be gone, back to its home in the tropical north.

She had heard people complain about the koel but Nabila was soothed by its song and would sometimes anticipate its *koo-eee*, clapping her hands in delight if she and the bird managed to synchronise their calls. The fact was, Nabila liked all birds, even the ones few others did. The swallows, the noisy miners, the pigeons, but most of all the white ibises, which had suddenly appeared in greater numbers a few summers ago, driven from their inland homes, enduring in spite of it all. One had recently started landing on her roof, heralding its arrival with an incongruous *honk*. *There is room enough for all living things*, believed Nabila Yasmeen.

Most mornings, in that tender space between slumber and sentience, Nabila Yasmeen summons memories of the village in which she was born.

She conjures an image of her house: two rooms formed from stone and mud with an arched door and a sprinkling of narrow holes for air and light. In the dark interior she spies the fireplace. On the wall around it are ladles and sieves and trays made of straw. On the shelf above it, clay pots full of olive oil, lentils, crushed wheat, rice and sugar. On the ground she sees the *batyeh*, the large wooden bowl in which her mother kneaded their daily bread. When she spins around she sees the wooden pegs in the walls where she used to hang her clothes. Next to these, the recesses where they stored the mattresses they slept on at night, and the curtain that covered the opening to keep the dust out. She feels the cool dry mud on which their mattresses lay, mud that her mother and sisters would have to fetch from the river every two weeks to make their floor new again.

Outside, she sees the roof of her house, curving in deference to the surrounding hills, echo barely discernible from source. In the cracks between the stones she sees the wild plants that, in springtime, blossomed into a tumbling extravagance of bright pink and yellow. To the right, a little way up the hill, she sees the *tabun*, the oven in which her mother and the other village women baked bread. She remembers lining up for that bread. She remembers the smell of it.

Even from this far away she can see the fields that circled the ancient village, drenched in yellow cactus blooms at the beginning of spring.

She feels the heat of the summer sun and the cool of the shade under the pomegranate trees. She can taste those pomegranates, and the figs and the almonds and the grapes, straight off the vine. She remembers the spring that provided them with water, for drinking, for washing, for play. She imagines hurling herself madly, joyfully, into the first autumn rains that signalled the end of the drought and the start of the olive harvest.

As if it were yesterday, she remembers the olive harvest, a time of pure, delicious happiness, when families gathered to pick *zaytoun* and picnic under the trees. She sees the colourful rugs spread under the branches, the ladders propped against the trunks, and the sacks and buckets dotting the ground, ready for filling. She hears the ululation in the women's song, the clapping of their hands and the beating of drums. She watches as long sticks coax the prized fruit from their branches.

She summons an image of her father and zeroes in on his face. She sees the scar that crossed the wrinkles under his right eye, the pores in his skin filled with black earth after a long day in the fields. She has no photograph of him but the tips of her fingers recall the rough, leathery surface of his skin. Try as she might, Nabila can't hear his voice but she remembers him dancing *dabke* at her eldest sister's wedding. She had thought him good-looking, with his strong, long nose and his prickly moustache. And the hairs in his ears that she would tickle to make him laugh.

She thinks of her mother, whose skin was the colour of grape molasses and whose hair turned white in the space of a day. She sees that hair in the long braid her mother would plait each morning and coil, clockwise, into a bun at the nape of her uncommonly long neck. The same technique she used to make baskets out of the unbroken stalks left over after the wheat had been threshed. Nabila imagines her mother, who would tickle her back at night to wind her down. 'Stop moving Nabila,' her mother would say, not in the language Nabila learnt to speak later but in the one she had first. 'Shhh Nabila, quiet now.' Each night they would lay together on the mattress, face to breast, fingers raising goosebumps, Nabila gently worrying her mother's earlobe until all movement stilled.

Often, Nabila would only pretend to be asleep so that she could watch her mother work late into the night, sewing *thobes* by the fluttering glow of a paraffin lamp. Later, she would decorate them with *tatreez*, stitch them meticulously with

14

threads of colourful silk. She wove histories lush with birds and flowers, feathers and trees. Sometimes, Nabila wonders if her mother's *thobes*, which would take weeks, even months, to complete, are worn by someone else now.

Nabila Yasmeen turned onto her side and pushed herself up with the heel of her small hand, now more avian than human. The arthritis that had crippled her mother before her had found its way into her joints now, swelling them and twisting her fingers in directions it didn't seem possible fingers could go. Slowly she shifted her hips so that her legs were no longer horizontal but hanging down towards the floor. It always took her a while to get moving so she steadied herself and looked down at the feet that dangled over her slippers. She stretched her toes, saw hard, yellow nails topping flat, lumpy paddles of flesh and bone that crawled with dark veins, the whole lot stretched over with skin so rough you could sand wood with it. She remembers a time when her feet didn't hold her back. When they didn't ache. When rising in the morning didn't mean waiting for her muscles to let go of her bones. When the simple act of moving one foot ahead of the other wasn't a painful reminder of the trees she used to climb and the hills she used to cross, but a joyous bridge between a curious child and a wonder-filled world.

In the bathroom, Nabila took off her glasses and moved her face as close to the mirror as it would go. Her neck, which once shot proudly upwards, was now fixed at an angle, forcing her eyes towards the floor. Nabila had never been beautiful but she remembers when there had been a clarity to her. Youth had drawn her dark and definite and now age was rubbing her out. People complained of wrinkles and sagging flesh but Nabila saw that growing old was more of a fading away. She turned on the cold tap, bent her head over the sink and splashed her face. Nabila was always careful not to use more water than she needed. She reached for the hand towel, dried her face and arranged her wiry hair with the edges of her fingernails. Delicately picking up her glasses so as not to dislodge the tape that held one of the arms in place, she put them back on and looked at the eyes that stared at her. The thick lenses may have made her eyes appear smaller, but they did not extinguish the fire that burnt bright behind them.

Her bed made tidy, her clothes on, Nabila shuffled through the dimly lit interior towards the light that penetrated her back window. She preferred the house dark, liked the solemnity of it. During those long hot summers in her village the blackness had countered the heat and brought with it a hush that soothed Nabila's busy mind.

From a container on the kitchen bench Nabila grabbed a handful of raisins and shovelled them greedily into her mouth. Her train of thought broken, she saw stubby fingers plucking grapes so precisely that a little stalk remained on each. She saw the grapes, slicked with oil, shimmering in the autumn sun, then brown and wrinkled after a few days in the mellow heat. And then smiled as she remembered the Feast of the Cross, celebrated throughout the land because it marked the end of the long, hot summer and the beginning of the blessed rains.

Nabila Yasmeen opened her back door to the garden she had nurtured through drought and flood. Suspended in an unbroken spider's web was an upside-down cicada, wings outstretched, like Icarus falling. She looked over at her neighbour's house, tutted and shook her head at the sight of the washing left on the line overnight. Again. And there were the magpies, three of them today, pecking at the ground for worms, the baby whining like a hungry child. In the distance she heard movement through the air. *There's the ibis*, she thought, as it swam through the clouds towards her, graceful in the sky. An altogether different creature up there.

While Nabila's small house held little more than what was needed for a simple life—no pictures hung on the walls and there were no shelves for books or photographs—her garden brimmed with life and colour. The peach and apricot trees, here when she moved in, were fruiting well. Nabila was pleased.

Circling Nabila's house were over a hundred pot plants, sentries on all fronts. She grew vegetables and herbs, and flowers that reminded her of home. Cyclamen and poppies, indigo and crocus. But she could never quite summon the courage to put them in the ground. She had lost count of how many there were but she knew them all, could remember exactly where they had come from, and cared for each without prejudice. Every morning she picked herbs for her tea—some sage, mint, lemon balm; maybe thyme, rosemary, basil, whatever was in season—ritually rubbing each between the fingers of her left hand and holding the leaves to her nose before placing them in a pot of water which she brought to the boil and drank once the liquid had reached the perfect temperature. Sitting at the windowsill in her back room, sipping her tea, she tended to her olive tree, begun as a cutting over fifty years ago and cultivated in bonsai form so that if Nabila had to leave the house her olive tree could leave with her. At the end of winter, she pruned it carefully, lifted it from its pot, trimmed its roots and settled it in again. She picked up her magnifying glass, checked for pests, then stroked the gnarly, miniature trunk with the tips of her wrinkled fingers, offering praise and smiling proudly at the new leaves that had uncurled overnight.

THREE

ثلاثة

Palestine, June 1948

There was nothing unusual about the morning of the day everything changed. It began as many other summer days had begun—with a clear sky and a warm breeze and the expectation that life would continue as ever it had, between the toiling of earth and the baking of bread.

Nabila yawned and stretched her arms above her head as she watched her family prepare for their day. It was just light but it was June, wheat harvest time, and there was much to be done. As her mother and father busied themselves gathering food and tools to take with them to the fields, her sisters headed for the village spring. '*Yallah habibti*,' she heard them say.

Barefoot, and still in her night clothes, Nabila crossed the raised threshold into the open air and squinted until her eyes grew accustomed to the golden light. She took the top off the *zir*, the large water jar that guarded the entrance to her house, and drank from its ample paunch.

'Do you know,' she said to the *zir*, as she grabbed two of its handles and looked into the face she imagined was there, 'that if you swallow the seeds of the watermelon, watermelons will grow out of your ears?'

Nabila thought that this was one of the funniest things she'd ever heard.

Not yet ready to find her sisters, because she knew they would make her bathe, Nabila said good morning to the goats, tickled them under their chins, and then lingered among the chickens that pecked at what they could find in the dry, stony ground. With her arms by her sides and her hands cupped upwards, she imitated their walk and scolded them for their transgressions.

Transitioning from fowl to mule, she flattened her heart-shaped palms on the hard ground and with an exaggerated *clip clop* and a loud, throaty *hee-haw*, she headed for the place that had enchanted her since the first time she had followed her sisters there—the village school. There was no one there that day, but she assumed her position beneath the window, because, she thought, *it was good to make sure*. All was quiet save for the whistle of a gentle wind and the rustle of sycamore leaves. In her peripheral vision she sensed movement. She turned her head slowly and right there, so close, was the most beautiful thing she'd ever seen. An enormous butterfly, yellow and black and blue with two perfectly round circles of red at the bottom of each wing, like eyes staring at her. From the distance came the sounds of the harvest.

When she had been at the window long enough to be convinced that indeed there would be no class today, Nabila headed in the direction of the main square where the old men of the village held court and where the *zajjal* was playing his *rababah*. She stopped for a while, hypnotised by the man's voice and the way he moved the bow back and forth over the single string.

I'm going to learn how to do that one day, said Nabila Yasmeen to herself.

Around the corner was Aziz's barber shop and to Nabila's delight there he was, the teacher, *her* teacher, having his hair cut. She loved visiting Aziz, he gave her sweets, and sometimes he would let her look inside the jar where he kept his leeches.

She approached the building slowly but neither man noticed her enter the shop. In the background someone was talking on the radio and Aziz and the teacher were deep in conversation, concerned expressions on their faces.

But then the barber looked up.

'Nabila my friend! Where are your shoes?'

'I forgot Aziz.'

'How many times do I have to tell you? You must not go without shoes. Or else I will have to put the leeches on you!' The barber laughed.

Nabila could watch the leeches all day, squirming in the rainwater, pebbles and moss that

Sara Haddad

was their home inside the jar. But having them on her skin was a different prospect entirely.

'I promise Aziz.'

She turned to the teacher, pulled on his sleeve and said, 'I want to learn to write my name.'

He looked at her, careful not to let his guard slip. He opened his mouth and then closed it again. He looked at his hands clasped in his lap.

'Aziz?'

He looked at the barber and then at Nabila.

'Do you have a piece of paper?'

Nabila beamed. Jumped up and down on her tiny toes. The teacher smiled.

Aziz fetched a scrap of paper and the teacher pulled his pen out of his pocket. It was plain and worn at the grip, where his fingers had rested year after year, but well weighted, and in a neat, clear script he wrote, slowly, from right to left:

نبيلة

Her hand sat lightly on his knee, her fingertips moving almost imperceptibly as he explained each letter to her. He told her that there were twenty-eight letters in the alphabet, *Al-abjadiyah*, but that her name only used a few of them. He then took her hand and placed it on his own, working her fingers into a grip around the pen. Like this they wrote her name, and wrote it again, and on the third attempt, he let her do it by herself. With her face only inches from the page, she slowly and determinedly copied his script, beaming with pride as she completed the last stroke.

'I did it!' she cried. 'I did it! I wrote my name!'

'Yes, Nabila, you did it. When the summer is over, you will be ready to come to school.' He laughed, and then abruptly stopped, and his face took on a troubled expression.

(In retrospect, Nabila realised, *as if he had been seized by a terrible thought*.)

Then he gave her the piece of paper and said, 'Go now, Nabila, your mother will be wondering where you are.'

With an extravagant sigh and a dramatic downward shrug of her shoulders, Nabila loped backwards out of the shop and continued on her way, the piece of paper firmly in her grip. Just out of town she approached the watchtower, below which they stored the grapes and figs at the end of summer. There was no one there so she got down on all fours and pretended she was a jackal infiltrating the fortress, secretly gorging on the delicious fruit. She imagined someone coming after her with a gun and ran down the hill in the direction of the spring.

When she finally arrived at her destination, her sisters were pounding the last of the wet clothes with the piece of wood they used to beat out the dirt. As usual they were giggling and teasing each other about the boys they liked. Who they were going to marry. How many children they would have. Nabila wondered why they couldn't talk about something more interesting, like the eagles she had seen circling the hills. Or the much-anticipated donkey her father had just bought. Bored by their silly chatter, she tiptoed along the tops of the rocks that circled the spring, wobbling on her bony feet, trying hard not to fall in. A strange hum sounded high in the sky and Nabila looked up at a bird she had never seen before. As she squatted to pick up a stone to throw into the water, she heard it and felt it and saw it all at once—the first of the bombs.

FOUR

أربعة

Australia, December 2023

There was no predicting the weather this week. Sweltering highs were followed by rains that washed the topsoil away, and woollens were retrieved from newly lined bottom drawers. Just yesterday, out popped a morning that was pure spring, a sweet, fresh chill in the air that said, *Let's have another go at this.*

But today's morning was one already drenched in cicada song, a horology of clocks being wound at once. Nabila watered her pots with the rainwater she had collected in all sorts of containers—old paint tins, watering cans, buckets, glass jars, all acquired for free from somewhere or other. She had grown accustomed to anticipating the needs of this garden, but in her village, over many centuries, the plants learned to grow in harmony with the seasons, and they never needed any more water than the rain that fell from the sky. Or the *nada* that fed the crops, made the earth so cool you could swear the fruit that was plucked off the trees had come straight from the fridge.

Nabila ventured to the bottom of her garden where parsley flourished among the weeds. Some, like the purslane they lived on in the months after their eviction, she picked for her morning omelette. Others, like the one they called asthma weed, she would wash and dry and pound to a coarse powder, which she would later make into a paste to apply to any burns or wounds that came her way. She tended to the plants that were beyond saving, not by pulling them out by the roots, but by digging them back into the soil.

Every day, before she went out, Nabila Yasmeen washed some of the clothes she had worn the day before, so that they would be dry and ready for her to wear again the next day. By hand in her bathroom sink she shifted fabric through soapy water, singing to herself the songs the women in the village used to sing as they washed their clothes in the stream by the spring, laughter interrupting song as news was exchanged and jokes were told. She wrung the water from her clothes, then took them out to the line that was strung up near her back door. One by one she shook the damp pieces as her mother had taught her, making sure to remove as many wrinkles as possible, before hanging them out to dry.

It was just after nine when Nabila left the house, first opening the wardrobe in her bedroom to collect her bag and her stick and her *keffiyeh*, which she folded once into a triangle and draped around her shoulders. Into the right-hand pocket of her corduroy trousers—which she wore all year round—she placed the stone she had carried with her for seventy-five years, the one she had picked up on the rocks near the spring and held tight in her hand the day the bombs fell. Every morning before going out she raised it to her nose, inhaled its earthy scent. If she closed her eyes tightly enough, and breathed in deeply enough, she could just catch the loamy smell that had once told them the spring rains were not far away. Into the pocket on the other side went the ancient black key that her mother used to close up their house for the very last time, almost everything they owned left inside, waiting for their return. Like Pompeii. Or the bedroom of a missing child.

The acrid scent of bush smoke hung in the still, mid-morning air. Copper-coloured skinks caught the heat on their backs and slithered over newly laid concrete, painfully bright and hot to the touch. Leaf shadows stencilled on the footpath offered sporadic relief from the sun. The low buzz of cicadas, interspersed with the strange, intermittent *knock knock knock* of an unseen frog, mingled with the distant sounds of traffic on the motorway.

The air was laden with moisture, the heat already sticking like fly paper. It clung to Nabila as a fractious child clings to her mother. Warm air filled her nostrils, made them hot. A hazy grey pall took the edge off all the outlines and made everything in the distance shimmer like a mirage. In the supermarket the day before she had heard people say that this would be the hottest summer on record, but Nabila didn't mind; she liked the heat. Nabila didn't read the newspapers and relied on snatches of conversation to keep her informed. She might scan the headlines outside the newsagent's for news of the world but found they rarely said anything interesting or important. Sometimes she watched the news on her television but it left so much out. And, much too often, was full of words and phrases like *alleged* and *apparent* and *according to*.

She stopped at the mini mart and treated herself to an ice cream. Staring into the freezer, trying to decide on a flavour, Nabila recalled the first ice cream she ever tasted. Mulberry. Tyrian purple with bright green pistachio nuts crushed on top. She was so very young, and her parents had taken her to visit her eldest brother who had secured an apprenticeship as a potter in the city. Bewildered by the cone she held in her hand, observing others in the shop eating theirs, she had looked up at her brother, eyes as wide as eyes could go, and said, 'Do I eat the whole thing?' She had never tasted anything like that ice cream, and she knew she never would again.

Nabila had been coming to Jamal's shop for many years now. They had spent hours reminiscing about their old countries, giving each other memories of places that were alike in so many ways. They exchanged stories of the otherness they had felt in their first years in the city they called home. They confessed to each other their embarrassment at being consigned to the back of the classroom with the other migrants who couldn't speak English. They had found a way to laugh about it but wondered at how they'd ever managed to learn anything at all. Nabila told Jamal about her first job, sewing cotton underwear for rich ladies in a grubby and dim-lit warehouse. She told him of the toll it had taken on her eyesight, which was never very good to begin with. And about the man she had hoped would share her life, but who turned out to be not what he seemed.

Between customers, they traded recipes and argued about the origin of *hummus*, how much lemon was a good amount, or how sweet the *marmoul* should be. In recent weeks Nabila had revealed more about her village to Jamal, how there was nothing left of it now, that all the houses had been demolished, the village renamed and new settlements built on the ruins and the bones of the dead. And beyond the new houses, pine forests, as far as the eye could see.

She described the different herbs and wildflowers she used to pick, the insects that would pollinate them, the animals and birds who had their open spaces taken away by bulldozers and Vested Interests and Divine Right. With great sorrow etched deep into the space between her brows, she told him of the millions of olive trees that had been destroyed, were still being cut down and burned, some of them thousands of years old. And of a people robbed of their livelihood and their dignity. But, she also told him, with an obdurate glimmer in her one good eye, 'What is above the land may be gone, but the roots hold on strong and deep.'

Through gentle eyes and with a soft voice, Jamal relayed the news as it was delivered. He told her the untellable, but he also told her that many people were marching, all over the world. That they'd had the biggest demonstration in London. He showed her pictures on his phone of crowds in Baghdad and Karachi, Santiago and Berlin. And he showed her images that she could never not see. Children being marched at gunpoint, tanks rolling over tents in refugee camps. Mothers writing the names of their babies on their limbs so that when they were blown up the bits of them, if found, might be buried together. Nabila saw the tears pool above the lower rims of Jamal's hazel eyes. She laid a reassuring hand on his quivering arm.

On her way to the bus stop Nabila noticed with relish the detritus that was stacked outside people's houses. There was almost nothing she enjoyed more than picking through the junk people discarded in a council clean-up. Most of it was useless, incomplete, or broken beyond repair, but Nabila found things others did not see. Like the handcrafted ladle that sat beside her stove and that she used in winter to make lentil soup. Or the curtains that had hung in a child's bedroom, a riotous menagerie that, apart from some fading and a few stains here and there, were perfectly good once she had given them a decent wash and left them to air in the sun for a while.

Once, to her amazement, she had found a woven tray, colours almost exactly like those in the trays the women carried on their heads at her sister's wedding. Deep red, eggplant purple, orange and green. Those trays were filled with fresh flowers and gifts, clothes, sweets, coffee. The tray Nabila found hangs near her back door and she uses it in summer to dry thyme and chillies.

If there is anything left tomorrow, thought Nabila Yasmeen, *I will come back and take a look.*

Nabila loved catching the bus. She knew all the drivers and made a point of always saying 'thank you' as she disembarked. Much of each day was spent on one number or another, travelling to and from the local shops, the doctor's surgery, or the park where the dogs went to play. In her handbag she carried a square piece of paper, folded twice and then twice again, worn on the creases from many openings and closings. On the paper were four maps in a row in various combinations of green and blue, a snapshot of dispossession. On the bus, during quieter parts of the day, and if she could identify a receptive ear, she would retrieve it from her handbag and begin to tell her story, the story of her sorrow, the sorrow she carried with her everywhere, all the time. Rarely would she find someone who was interested and willing to listen for very long. Most people were kind, they would manage a smile, but then move seats, or turn away and look out the window, or bring out their phone and start scrolling, anxious for the journey to end.

But last week she had sat next to a young man and his girlfriend who were headed where she was. Not only were they *interested* in her story, they *understood*, told her things even she didn't know. *Maybe things are changing*, thought Nabila Yasmeen.

Nabila stepped off the bus to a loud crack in the menacing sky. Angry clouds sat heavy on the horizon, their gun–metal grey bellies swollen with indignation. Vertical sheets of charcoal suggested rain was not far away. Lightning in the distance flashed and great rolling engines rumbled high in the air.

The birds went quiet and the light went away.

Hail the size of chickpeas turned the ground white, then melted into rain spots fat with water and relief. Soon the downpour was so heavy that Nabila had no choice but to stop and wait. She took shelter outside a bread shop, under a sign marked with the language of others who had also been displaced. As she stood there she noticed a flyer that had been stuck to the glass on the bus stop opposite. It said, 'Jesus Is Coming. Are You Ready?'

Nabila's heart was brave and true, but her faith ... her faith, well, that was another thing altogether. Deprived of water and light, it had gradually wilted and dried. Jesus, born a stone's throw from her village, had turned out to be a tremendous disappointment. As for His Father, she had trouble convincing herself that an all-powerful being could allow the lives of so many innocent children to be taken, savagely, cruelly, repeatedly. She couldn't fathom how people could speak of holiness and do despicable things. How they could worship a god who favoured the strong over the weak. Nabila Yasmeen was not afraid to speak her mind and she thought that if indeed Jesus was coming again (as they said He was) that she'd have quite a lot to say to Him.

The rain gone and the air clear of the humidity that had engulfed her, Nabila continued on her way. An almighty roar caused her to freeze and then duck as the engines of the passenger jet reverberated overhead. The planes flew so low to the ground here that Nabila felt she could almost see the faces of the people staring through the windows as the plane came in to land. When the planes hovered over her village seventy-five years ago, delivering menace and blight, they were almost as loud.

FIVE

خمسة

Palestine, June 1948

As she rushed back from the spring, with the stone she had been about to throw in one hand and the piece of paper with her name on it in the other, another bomb fell from the sky and landed on the ground, bringing with it an almighty *BOOM!* that sent Nabila's little frame flying into the air. Her head and body shook with pain, and blood ran down the left side of her face.

'Get up, Nabila, run!' someone shouted. She didn't know whose voice it was or where the voice was coming from. It seemed to Nabila that she lay on the ground for a very long time. When she came to, a woman was crouched over her, brushing the dust from her body, drizzling water onto her face. 'Wake up Nabila, are you alright? Can you hear me?' Nabila had such a sore head but the woman helped her up and led her by the hand towards the road that snaked away from the village. The stone was stuck fast to her palm but the piece of paper with her name on it was nowhere to be seen. For three days she stayed with the woman and her family. They fed her, kept her warm and tended to her wounds. Cared for her until her father found her, his slight frame shuddering with relief, his tears hot, soaking her head as her held her close.

After the bombs came the soldiers, and they bore mortars, machine guns and a directive from God. For two months Nabila and her family sheltered under the olive trees between her village and the next, and then in a cave as the soldiers drove them further away. Air raids and shelling made it impossible for them to return, but in the days after they were forced from their home, Nabila's mother and sisters snuck back into the village at night to retrieve whatever they could and bring it back to the camp. Eggs from the chickens, blankets, clothes, fruit stolen from their own trees. They built fires with sticks and crushed olive pits, to cook over and to keep them warm. They foraged for weeds that grew between the trees and the cracks in the stone walls.

As the weeks passed they were joined by families from other villages who told them that the same thing had happened to them. That even with white flags raised, men had been rounded up and shot, and thrown into ditches while their families looked on. Some described how kerosene had been poured onto their food stores and burned. Others told them how they'd been marched out of their villages at gunpoint and forced to watch as soldiers set fire to their houses. All spoke of terror and of their wish to go home.

One man arrived from the city, and gave them news from further away. He told of how the water supply in Akka had been poisoned with typhoid. He brought news of a passenger train that had been blown up near Tulkarm. He told of murders and rapes and crimes committed by soldiers who had come from somewhere else. How in Lydda and Deir Yassin and Ramla they had massacred hundreds of people. Left them decapitated and disembowelled. And how, in Yafa, they had hidden explosives under oranges in a truck and blown it up in front of a shop in a busy part of town. He mimicked the way they would drive trucks through towns, shooting bullets at pedestrians as they went. Nabila stared, wide-eyed, horrified, hypnotised by the images playing out in her head.

By the time autumn had set in they had moved on again, their early hopes of returning to their village crushed. They went on foot through difficult mountain terrain, with others who had nowhere to go. The land was strewn with bombs and bodies. One man had brought his sheep and nothing else. Some people carried bags of wheat on their heads. Many only had the keys to their houses and the clothes they stood up in. On bleeding feet they walked out of their country into a desolate future.

SIX

ستة

Australia, December 2023

Nabila didn't normally take the train but it was the fastest and most direct way of getting to the city. And she had come to look forward to the journey, weekly now. She enjoyed the gentle sideways rocking of the train, which was different to the sometimes violent rock and lurch of the bus. She always sat on the left side of the carriage and made a point of finding something new through the window each time.

Sometimes the train was full, but today it was not. At one of the stations a woman got on and walked towards her to sit down, but then glanced at Nabila's *keffiyeh* and walked through the door to the next car.

Nabila scanned the carriage to see how many other people might be coming to the march and caught the eye of a young boy who promptly lowered his head and turned to his mother, shyly pointing and whispering about the badge that was pinned to Nabila's chest. Emboldened by this symbol of her solidarity, he turned his face towards her again and smiled. Right there in front of her his spine seemed to galvanise and grow straighter. *He's on holidays*, she thought, and then her knees weakened at the realisation that many thousands of children would never even start school, let alone return for a new term.

The train dipped and plunged into the darkness and the voices within the carriage, now encased within the tunnel, clamoured and grew sharper. Nabila was deaf in one ear and the concentration and intensity of the noise was almost unbearable.

Nabila craned her neck as high as it would go and watched as the front of the train came into view, curving its way through the receding darkness. To her left she spied water through palm trees, the inevitable cruise ship, and the peninsula on which a man called Bennelong, whose land was also stolen, once lived. As far as she could see, the only clue that this land was his was the red, yellow and black flag that flickered in the breeze.

At the station with the tunnel that had once been converted into an air raid shelter, Nabila alighted from the train with the boy and his family. She read on one of the posters that this had been done during the Second World War, but the shelter had never been used. *How strange to have air raid shelters but no bombs*, thought Nabila Yasmeen.

In the tunnel she passed a man in a sleeping bag and there was no way of knowing if he was dead or alive. She dropped a coin into his cup, just in case.

The sun was at its most intense and Nabila suddenly felt very tired. Over the weeks she had been coming here, more and more stalls had been set up along the edges of the path that led to the fountain, selling badges, bracelets, T-shirts and refreshments, to raise money for those in need. Or for those who saw an opportunity to make a quick profit. Some people wanted her to sign petitions, or handed out flyers promoting political ideologies, but Nabila Yasmeen wasn't interested in any of these. She brushed them all off as she shuffled her way to the edge of the fountain to steady her legs and catch her shallow breath.

As the call to prayer sounded she watched people make their way from all directions to gather in the shade of the fig trees. Some wore the *keffiyeh* on their heads; others, like her, had the scarf, black and white and other colours too, draped over their shoulders. Flags of all sizes and flags from other countries rippled in the breeze and people held placards above their heads, placards that called for justice and freedom. From her place in the sun Nabila felt the air inflate her lungs, and the shadow recede from around her heart. She would sometimes try to make eye contact with people as they walked past her and, if she did, she nodded and smiled and they would nod and smile too.

Nabila stood up and walked towards one of the benches under the trees. It was too hot to remain in the sun. Under dappled light a man had set up an easel and was painting the scene. Fire engine sirens wailed in the distance and she detected in the crowd, for the first time since the marches had begun, a weariness that had nothing to do with the heat. She opened her bag and pulled out the *saj* she had bought from Jamal. She took a bite and then another as she locked eyes with an ibis striding purposefully towards her. Old man strut on skinny old man legs. *This is not for you*, murmured Nabila Yasmeen.

Mournful music, heavy with sorrow, played through a large speaker that had been set up near the fountain. In front of her on the grass children blew bubbles through a portable machine. As the speakers began so did the Cathedral's bells, ringing long and loud, but neither the bells nor the aggressive *chop chop chop* of the police helicopter's blades above quelled the stiffening resolve of the crowd.

A belligerent wind bullied its way through the park, upsetting the fountain's symmetry but giving full expression to the flags people waved above their heads. Today, Nabila was sure, the wind was on their side.

The call to march brought Nabila to her feet. For the last two months she had come here every week and this is what she came for, to sound her voice with the voices of others. To join her cry with the cries of those whose pain and anger were deepening at the incomprehensible refusal to condemn. She looked around at all the faces, some familiar, many new. She saw skin and hair in every shade, faces from all continents, many nations. In front of her a woman juggled a sign, a handbag and a sleeping child. People approached the woman, asking if she needed help. *There are so many good people here today*, thought Nabila Yasmeen. She wondered if that was enough.

Slowly the crowd began to move, joined at the tail by another and another and another until the procession was complete and the colours of the watermelon filled the air. As the march gained momentum Nabila felt everything inside her swell. *From where in the deep well of grief*, thought Nabila Yasmeen, *does such love spring?*

The protest route changed from week to week and today it took them past the designer shops. 'While you're shopping, bombs are dropping.' In other weeks they were flanked by the park, which Nabila preferred, favouring the company of trees to that of expensive handbags. 'In our thousands, in our millions.' But mostly she liked the other route better because it took them under the stone arch and for a couple of glorious minutes, as the voices coalesced and echoed an almighty cry of 'Ceasefire Now! Ceasefire Now!', it was possible to believe that the whole world was contained within that space and everyone in it said, 'Yes, I see now.'

Ordinarily Nabila went straight home after the march but today she had other plans; tonight she would attend a vigil to mourn and remember the dead. More than twenty thousand at last count, almost half of them children. For Nabila Yasmeen and millions of others, the Nakba was the beginning and the end of everything. Only it had never ended. More than seventy-five years and seventy-five days later it endured. More brutal than ever.

The park she arrived at in the evening was smaller than the one she had grown used to, with more open space and enormous plane trees lining just one side. In their canopies screeched what sounded to Nabila like thousands of rainbow lorikeets, at least one for each of the dead, their deafening squawks competing for air space with the whine of the cicadas, and all of them, birds and insects, a chaos of toddlers protesting the unfairness of it all.

Below the trees, around the edge of the park on concrete steps almost as tall as Nabila herself, twenty thousand lights flickered. There was a candle for each soul, with coloured ones for the children. Nabila followed the crowd and did as they did. Formed her index and middle fingers into a V and raised her arm above her head. A Darug elder performed a smoking ceremony and the sharp eucalyptus burn caught the tears that lodged in the back of her throat. She willed them away.

Out here, in the open air, in the company of nature and a respectful hush, listening to the words of the priest and the rabbi and the imam, imagining Bethlehem silent this Christmas, Nabila felt as close to God as she had in a long time.

As she heard that it would take over eight hours to read out the names and ages of all the dead, she looked up and saw four ibises flying in formation and offered a prayer to the darkening sky.

Time to go home, said Nabila Yasmeen to herself.

SEVEN

سبعة

Palestine, August 1948

Once upon a time, Nabila Yasmeen had spent much of each day off the ground. A skinny fledgling with large knees and wiry coils of unruly hair, it had been her job to climb to the very top of the olive trees and pick the sweetest fruit, which her mother would crush under a stone and pickle in brine with lemon and chilli peppers.

After her wounds had healed, when they were still within walking distance of their village,

Nabila would make her way to the woods near her house and watch as the animals grazed and the fruit on the trees rotted in the accelerating heat. When the wind blew in the right direction she could smell the *za'atar* and longing clutched at her chest.

Because a place under the window was now impossible, sometimes Nabila would climb the sycamores that ringed the school, their thick foliage cloaking her tiny frame. It was from this place in the trees that she watched the teacher guard the door to the classroom, the veins in his hands bulging as he clutched a battered and rusty old rifle, a British relic from World War Two, secured in exchange for his wife's wedding ring, and about as effective as stones against a tank.

Nabila was six-and-a-quarter years old, almost, when he was murdered. She never did get to sit at one of those desks, or find out what happened after the first lesson. Her enduring memory of him is not the one she thought she would have. The truth is, she prefers not to remember the last time she saw him: lying in a circle of blood at the entrance to the school, bullet holes spoiling the skin on his precious neck.

EIGHT

ثمانية

Australia, December 2023

It had been a long day and Nabila's small body was dense with fatigue. The brief storm had stripped the gloom from the clouds which were now sparse, and lighter and higher in the sky. Between spider silk swirls beamed the moon. It pulled Nabila as it pulls the tides, always one step ahead.

Nabila Yasmeen turned the last corner on her long journey back and made her way slowly up the gradual incline that led to her house. Frangipani flowers, blasted from fat finger-like branches during the storm, reflected the moonlight, yellow-centred stars lighting her way. The air was still, quiet, save for the alarm-like call of a tawny frogmouth and the sound of someone practising their saxophone in a flat behind a window on the second floor. Suddenly she was filled with an ache so profound and so intense that the hope that had grown inside her over the course of the day cowered and then fled like a timorous child. It wasn't that she didn't like the music, no that wasn't it at all. It was just that it came from somewhere she didn't and she wished, oh how she wished, that she could hear the twang of the *rababah* just one more time.

Reaching her front door, Nabila retrieved her house key from the inside top pocket of her handbag, inserted it into the lock and pushed down on the handle. She switched on the light, propped her stick up in the corner of her room, put down her bag and took off her *keffiyeh*. The house was stuffy from being closed up all day, so she walked to her back room and opened the window, and she was sure she saw her little olive tree thank her for it.

She was almost too tired to eat but reached into the fridge and pulled out a bowl of *labneh*, which she picked at with some bread and ate while sipping the rest of the tea she had made that morning. Through the open window drifted the breeze and cricket song and the secrets of the night.

In her bedroom, Nabila pulled back the sheets and drew the blind down, but not all the way. She reached into her pockets, right then left, and pulled out her stone and the old black key. Onto each she bestowed a delicate kiss and returned them to their places in the wardrobe.

Until next week, whispered Nabila Yasmeen.

ADDENDUM

The story of Nabila Yasmeen is fictional, but the events that took place in Palestine in 1947 and 1948[1] and which are told in her story are based on the oral and written histories of those who were forced to leave their homes during *Al Nakba*, 'the catastrophe'.

Noam Chomsky said, 'The last paradox is that the tale of Palestine from the beginning until today is a simple story of colonialism and dispossession,

---

1 The same year the General Assembly of the United Nations adopted the Universal Declaration of Human Rights.

yet the world treats it as a multifaceted and complex story—hard to understand and even harder to solve.'[2] While the fate of the indigenous people of Palestine was undoubtedly sealed on 2 November 1917 with the Balfour Declaration—a brief letter from the British foreign secretary to Lord Rothschild which promised to the Zionist movement 'the establishment in Palestine of a national home for the Jewish people'[3]—the story had in fact begun some thirty years earlier: with the establishment and rise of political Zionism in late-19th-century Europe.

Until 1918, for just over 400 years, Palestine had been under the rule of the Ottoman Empire. In the mid-19th century, when the population numbered around 500,000, more than 80 percent

2   Chomsky, N. and Pappé, I. (2015), *On Palestine*, Penguin Books, London.

3   https://avalon.law.yale.edu/20th_Century/balfour.asp

were Muslim, 10 percent were Christian Arabs and 5 to 7 percent were Jewish.[4] During this time, the population coexisted in relative peace.

In 1923, The League of Nations established the British Mandate for Palestine to place 'the country under such political, administrative and economic conditions as will secure the establishment of the Jewish national home, as laid down in the preamble, and the development of self-governing institutions, and also for safeguarding the civil and religious rights of all the inhabitants of Palestine, irrespective of race and religion'.[5]

From 1923 to 1947, the situation in Palestine grew progressively worse for the indigenous population. British colonialism combined with large-scale Jewish immigration, mostly of Jewish

---

4   Lughod (1971, p. 140).
5   https://avalon.law.yale.edu/20th_century/palmanda.asp

people from Europe who were fleeing Nazism, increased tensions and Palestinian resistance, which ultimately led to the Arab Revolt of 1936–1939. During this time British airplanes bombed villages, imposed curfews and enacted collective punishment on the Palestinian population.[6] The British began demolishing Palestinian houses and forcibly displacing people, a practice that Zionist forces continued and which Israel carries out to this day.[7] Five thousand Palestinians were killed, more than 15,000 were wounded and 5,600 were imprisoned.[8]

On 29 November 1947, the United Nations (UN) passed Resolution 181, which recommended the partition of Palestine into

---

6 https://ciaotest.cc.columbia.edu/journals/jps/v39i2/f_0025895_21187.pdf

7 https://www.npr.org/2024/03/23/1236628495/israel-settlers-attack-west-bank-palestinians-settlement-outposts

8 https://www.palquest.org/en/highlight/158/great-arab-revolt-1936-1939

Arab and Jewish states. At this time Palestinians comprised 67 percent of the population and owned 93 percent of the land.[9] The plan was rejected by the Arab High Committee on the basis that it gave over half of Palestine, including most of the fertile coastal region, to a group of people who were mostly newly arrived European immigrants.[10] David Ben-Gurion, who would become Israel's first prime minister, said the borders of the new state would 'be determined by force and not by the partition resolution'.[11]

In the same year, Zionist forces, which had been importing arms and building weapons factories, began destroying Palestinian towns and villages and expelling people from their homes.[12]

---

9 https://www.un.org/unispal/history2/origins-and-evolution-of-the-palestine-problem/part-i-1917-1947/

10 https://www.un.org/unispal/document/auto-insert-202927/

11 Pappe (2007, p. 37).

12 https://www.washingtonpost.com/history/2023/11/03/israel-nakba-history-1948/

On 14 May 1948, the British Mandate expired and Ben-Gurion declared the establishment of the state of Israel.

From 1947 to 1949, some 530 Palestinian villages, towns and cities were depopulated or destroyed in the Nakba,[13,14] with Zionist forces capturing 78 percent of historic Palestine. Today, pine trees 'cover many of the destroyed Palestinian villages, hiding their remains under vast "green lungs" planted by the Jewish National Fund for the purpose of "recreation and tourism"'.[15]

The remaining 22 percent of historic Palestine comprised what is now known as the West Bank and the Gaza Strip, which were later occupied by Israel in the 1967 Six-Day War.

---

13 https://reliefweb.int/report/occupied-palestinian-territory/israeli-apartheid-legacy-ongoing-nakba-75-enar

14 https://www.un.org/unispal/document/auto-insert-202927/

15 https://yplus.ps/wp-content/uploads/2021/01/Pappe-Ilan-The-Ethnic-Cleansing-of-Palestine.pdf

During the Nakba, around 15,000 Palestinians were killed and more than 750,000 people, almost three-quarters of the Palestinian population, were displaced.[16] Today these people and their descendants number around 15 million, about 7 million of whom live in poverty in refugee camps and are subject to repeated human rights abuses and violations.[17] In 2018, 70 percent of the population of Gaza were internally displaced refugees.[18]

During the Nakba, Zionist forces and their supporters 'collected' tens of thousands of Palestinian books. 'Thousands of the books were recycled into paper while others were absorbed into the National Library of Israel's general collection, making it impossible to trace

16 https://greens.org.au/news/speech/speech–nakba–catastrophe
17 https://www.refugeesinternational.org/palestine–israel/
18 https://www.ochaopt.org/sites/default/files/gaza_thematic_6_0.pdf

them today ... Each book bears the label "AP" (abandoned property).'[19]

In December 1948, the UN General Assembly passed Resolution 194, which called for the right of return for Palestinian refugees. Israel's admittance as a member of the UN in May 1949 was conditional on its acceptance of Resolution 194, which it has yet to implement.

In 2011, the Israeli Knesset passed the Nakba Law, which cut state funding to any organisation 'that commemorates the Palestinian Nakba, studies, mentions or produces knowledge about it'.[20]

In 2015, the Palestine Sunbird (*Nectarinia Osea*) was named the national bird of Palestine and, despite its small size, is one of the most enduring symbols of Palestinian resistance.

---

19 https://www.972mag.com/documenting-scores-of-palestinian-books-nakbas-lesser-known-victims/

20 Abdo and Masalha (2019, p. 297).

Representing beauty and freedom of movement, it feeds on the nectar of flowers, in particular jasmine.

Israel's latest military assault on Gaza, which has had the full support of the United States and other Western governments, is the fifth and most devastating. In less than one month, Israel dropped the equivalent of two nuclear bombs on the Gaza Strip,[21] which is 'tiny, cramped and as densely populated as London'.[22]

Since 2007, the Gaza Strip has been under an Israeli air, sea and land blockade. Since then, and before 2023, there had been four protracted periods of aggression on the 41-kilometre-long strip of land—in 2008, 2014, 2018 and 2021.

---

21 Euro-Med Human Rights Monitor https://euromedmonitor.org/ en/article/5908/Israel-hits-Gaza-Strip-with-the-equivalent-of-two-nuclear-bombs

22 https://apnews.com/article/israel-gaza-hamas-war-90e02d26420b8fe3 157f73c256f9ed6a

Over a period of some fifteen years, tens of thousands of Palestinians have been killed, most of them children and women. Homes, hospitals, schools, office buildings and places of worship have been destroyed. With every assault, rebuilding has been difficult as the years-long siege prevents construction materials from reaching Gaza.

The events of late 2023 and 2024 have widely been referred to as a second Nakba.[23] On 13 October 2023, 'Israeli authorities ordered more than a million people in northern Gaza to evacuate their homes. Two months later, almost 1.9 million people—85 percent of Gaza's population—are displaced, nearly half crammed inside Rafah, the enclave's southernmost governorate with a pre-

---

23 https://www.haaretz.com/israel-news/2023-11-12/ty-article/
    israeli-security-cabinet-member-calls-north-gaza-evacuation-nakba-
    2023/0000018b-c2be-dea2-a9bf-d2be7b670000

war population of 280,000.'[24] On 6 May 2024, Israel began a military offensive in and around the city of Rafah.

As at January 2024, 25,295 people had been killed and 63,000 injured. Two million two hundred thousand people were at immediate risk of famine, while 378,000 were at the catastrophic 'Phase 5' level—starvation and exhaustion of coping capacities. Six hundred and twenty-five thousand children—100 percent of the remaining child population—had no access to education.[25]

At the beginning of 2024, around 80 percent of buildings in northern Gaza had been destroyed,[26] including through the bombing of hospitals, ambulances, schools, universities, refugee camps,

---

24 https://www.hrw.org/news/2023/12/20/most-gazas-population-remains-displaced-and-harms-way

25 https://www.ochaopt.org/content/hostilities-gaza-strip-and-israel-reported-impact-day-107

26 https://truthout.org/articles/with-70-percent-of-gaza-homes-destroyed-biden-approves-147m-israel-arms-sale/

mosques and churches. In addition to over 9,000 children, those killed included health workers, journalists and humanitarian aid workers. Many more dead lay beneath the rubble, and clean water, food, fuel, electricity and medical supplies were denied. As at February 2024, at least 17,000 children had been orphaned[27] and another 1,000 disabled.[28] As in 2008, Israel deployed internationally banned weaponry, such as white phosphorous.[29] By late April 2024, the situation had deteriorated considerably.

For more than 75 years the Nakba has determined the lives of the vast majority of Palestinians. It represents not only the loss of home and land but loss of 'archives, libraries, public

---

27 https://www.telegraph.co.uk/global-health/terror-and-security/gaza-17000-orphans-palestine-israel-hamas-war/

28 https://www.cbc.ca/news/world/gaza-amputees-children-1.7093914

29 https://www.hrw.org/news/2023/10/12/israel-white-phosphorus-used-gaza-lebanon

buildings, archaeological treasures, and the rupture of national institutions and identity'.[30] Thus, the Nakba is 'not past but ongoing, manifested in the occupation itself, settlement construction, in killings that are not investigated or punished, illegal detention, torture, home demolitions, land grabs and community evictions'.[31]

Recent events in the Gaza Strip have seen most people's homes destroyed and the population driven further and further south, with increasingly fewer places to go.

On 26 January 2024 the International Court of Justice 'ordered "immediate and effective measures" to protect Palestinians in the occupied Gaza Strip from the risk of genocide by ensuring sufficient humanitarian aid and enabling basic services', but 'Israel has continued to disregard

---

30 Abdo and Masalha (2019, p. 115).
31 Ibid., p. 126.

its obligation as the occupying power to ensure the basic needs of Palestinians in Gaza are met'.[32]

On 18 March 2024, EU foreign policy chief Josep Borrell said, 'In Gaza we are no longer on the brink of famine, we are in a state of famine … This is unacceptable. Starvation is used as a weapon of war.'[33]

Ben-Gurion said in reference to the Palestinians, 'The old will die and the young will forget.'[34] Golda Meir said, 'It was not as if there was a Palestinian people in Palestine and we came and threw them out and took their country away from them. They did not exist.'[35]

Neither of these statements is true.

---

32 https://www.amnesty.org.au/israel-defying-icj-ruling-to-prevent-genocide-by-failing-to-allow-adequate-humanitarian-aid-to-gaza/

33 https://www.reuters.com/world/middle-east/eus-borrell-says-israel-is-provoking-famine-gaza-2024-03-18/

34 https://www.progressiveisrael.org/ben-gurions-notorious-quotes-their-polemical-uses-abuses/

35 https://www.jewishvirtuallibrary.org/golda-meir-quotes-on-israel-and-judaism

POSTSCRIPT

At the time of releasing this new edition of *The Sunbird*, in late 2024, there was still no ceasefire in the Gaza Strip and the situation remains catastrophic. On 24 April 2024, Euro-Med Human Rights Monitor estimated that approximately 70,000 tons of bombs had been dropped on Gaza, 'far surpassing the [bombing] of Dresden, Hamburg, and London combined during World War II'.[36] The military bombardment has been relentless, resulting in acute physical and psychological destruction

36 https://www.aa.com.tr/en/middle-east/amount-of-israeli-bombs-dropped-on-gaza-surpasses-that-of-world-war-ii/3239665

that is multifaceted and multidimensional in nature. Continuous evacuation orders have resulted in 90 percent of the population being displaced at least once, 'if not up to 10 times',[37] often to designated 'safe zones', only to be bombed as they seek shelter in tents, schools and hospitals.

On 14 June 2024, the G7 leaders of Canada, France, Germany, Italy, Japan, the UK and the US released a statement that said: 'We express our full solidarity and support to Israel and its people and reaffirm our unwavering commitment towards its security.'[38] On 29 August 2024, in the US, AIPAC (the American Israel Public Affairs Committee) officially surpassed $100 million in donations to both the Republican and

---

37 https://www.theguardian.com/world/article/2024/jul/03/about-90-of-people-in-gaza-displaced-since-war-began-says-un-agency

38 https://www.whitehouse.gov/briefing-room/statements-releases/2024/06/14/g7-leaders-statement-8/

Democratic parties for the 2024 presidential elections.[39]

On 2 July 2024, Shin Bet revealed that 21,000 Palestinian prisoners were being held in Israeli jails.[40] A report by the UN Human Rights Office, published on 31 July 2024, 'covers allegations of torture and other forms of cruel, inhuman and degrading treatment, including sexual abuse of women and men ... The staggering number of men, women, children, doctors, journalists and human rights defenders detained since 7 October, most of them without charge or trial and held in deplorable conditions, along with reports of ill-treatment and torture and violation of due process guarantees, raises serious concerns regarding

---

39 https://readsludge.com/2024/08/27/aipac-officially-surpasses-100-million-in-spending-on-2024-elections/

40 https://thecradle.co/articles-id/25732

the arbitrariness and the fundamentally punitive nature of such arrests and detention', said UN Human Rights Chief Volker Türk.[41]

On 17 July 2024, in a report to the UN General Assembly, Michael Fakhri, UN Special Rapporteur on the Right to Food, said, 'Never in post-war history had a population been made to go hungry so quickly and so completely as was the case for the 2.3 million Palestinians living in Gaza', and that Israel has used starvation in Gaza 'with the intent to destroy in whole or in part the Palestinian people'.[42]

On 19 July 2024, the International Court of Justice (ICJ) 'declared that Israel's occupation of the Gaza strip and the West Bank, including East Jerusalem, is unlawful, along with the associated

---

41 https://www.ohchr.org/en/press-releases/2024/07/un-report-palestinian-detainees-held-arbitrarily-and-secretly-subjected

42 https://www.un.org/unispal/document/right-to-food-report-17jul24/

settlement regime, annexation and use of natural resources. The Court added that Israel's legislation and measures violate the international prohibition on racial segregation and apartheid. The ICJ mandated Israel to end its occupation, dismantle its settlements, provide full reparations to Palestinian victims and facilitate the return of displaced people.'[43]

On 25 July 2024, at the invitation of the Republican majority in the House of Representatives, Israeli prime minister Benjamin Netanyahu addressed US Congress for the fourth time in his career. He said, 'Give us the tools faster and we'll finish the job faster.'[44] He received a standing ovation.

---

43 https://www.ohchr.org/en/press-releases/2024/07/experts-hail-icj-declaration-illegality-israels-presence-occupied

44 https://www.jewishnews.co.uk/netanyahu-invokes-churchill-in-speech-to-congress-urging-give-us-the-tools-and-well-finish-the-job/

On 25 August 2024, the World Health Organization confirmed that a ten-month-old baby in Gaza had become paralysed by polio, the first case to have been recorded in the area in more than 25 years.[45] While the polio vaccine was administered in early September to around 560,000 children in the first round of the UN campaign,[46] other diseases continue to spread, including diseases of the skin, 'such as scabies, rashes, and chickenpox, attributed to the dire conditions in overcrowded displacement camps'.[47] In addition, normally preventable diseases and conditions such as Hepatitis A, diarrhoea and respiratory infections are widespread and may have 'fatal or debilitating

45 https://www.wired.com/story/how-did-polio-reemerge-in-gaza-after-a-quarter-of-a-century-virologist/

46 https://news.un.org/en/story/2024/09/1154311

47 https://www.dci-palestine.org/_covered_in_blisters_chickenpox_and_other_skin_diseases_spread_among_palestinian_children_in_gaza_amid_israeli_genocide

consequences given the current state of health care'.[48] Cholera, measles and meningococcal meningitis 'pose a mortal threat'[49] as piles of rubbish grow higher next to tents and shelters, sewage floods the streets and access to hygiene products is limited.

UNICEF Global Spokesperson James Elder called the Gaza Strip 'the most dangerous place in the world to be a child'.[50] In March 2024, Ghassan Abu-Sittah, a London-based plastic-and-reconstructive surgeon who specialises in paediatric trauma, said, 'This is the biggest cohort of pediatric amputees in history.'[51] Many amputations are performed without anaesthetic. Doctors report

---

48 https://www.rescue.org/press-release/irc-emergency-team-warns-public-health-catastrophe-underway-gaza
49 Ibid.
50 https://www.unicef.org/press-releases/unicef-geneva-palais-briefing-note-gaza-worlds-most-dangerous-place-be-child
51 https://www.newyorker.com/news/dispatch/the-children-who-lost-limbs-in-gaza

that 'many of the deaths, amputations and life changing wounds to children they have treated came from the firing of missiles and shells—in areas crowded with civilians—packed with additional metal designed to fragment into tiny pieces of shrapnel'.[52] Moreover, a majority of 'operations were on children hit by small pieces of shrapnel that leave barely discernible entry wounds but create extensive destruction inside the body. Amnesty International has said that the weapons appear designed to maximise casualties.'[53] In early July 2024, it was estimated that between 15,000 and 25,000 children had lost at least one parent, signalling a crisis that will 'haunt Gaza for years to come'.[54]

---

52 https://www.theguardian.com/world/article/2024/jul/11/israeli-weapons-shrapnel-children-gaza-injured

53 Ibid.

54 https://www.lemonde.fr/en/international/article/2024/07/04/gazan-orphans-face-suffering-beyond-territory-s-borders_6676664_4.html

As the new school year began in much of the world, most youth and adults in Gaza, which boasts one of the highest literacy rates in the world,[55] are beginning their second year without school or university. According to Save the Children International, as at April 2024, 87.7% of all school buildings in Gaza had been damaged or destroyed.[56]

Israel's war on Gaza has also been lethal for aid workers, healthcare workers and journalists. 'The war in Gaza has no 21st-century precedent that can approach the sheer carnage it has brought on humanitarians. More than 200 aid workers have been killed in seven months—exceeding the total number killed in the entire world in any year in the past two decades.'[57] Regarding healthcare

---

55 https://www.undp.org/sites/g/files/zskgke326/files/migration/ps/
    UNDP-papp-research-PHDR2015Education.pdf

56 https://www.savethechildren.net/blog/education-under-attack-
    gaza-nearly-90-school-buildings-damaged-or-destroyed

57 https://reliefweb.int/report/occupied-palestinian-territory/gazas-
    invisible-massacre-aid-workers-killed-record-numbers

workers, 'The UN Human Rights Office decries the reported killing of 500 health workers [which] have occurred against the backdrop of systematic attacks on hospitals and other medical facilities in violation of the laws of war.'[58] As at 13 September 2024, the Committee to Protect Journalists' (CPJ) preliminary investigations showed at least 116 journalists and media workers had been killed, making it the 'deadliest period for journalists since CPJ began gathering data in 1992'.[59]

The Israeli assault on Gaza has created a volume of debris that is fourteen times greater than the combined total from all conflicts across the world since 2008.[60] In terms of climate,

---

58 https://www.un.org/unispal/document/statement-gaza-ohchr-25jun24/

59 https://cpj.org/2024/09/journalist-casualties-in-the-israel-gaza-conflict/

60 https://unitar.org/about/news-stories/news/gaza-debris-generated-current-conflict-14-times-more-combined-sum-all-debris-generated-other

research has revealed that '[t]he planet-warming emissions generated during the first two months of the war in Gaza were greater than the annual carbon footprint of more than 20 of the world's most climate-vulnerable nations'.[61]

As at 13 September 2024, 41,118 people have been killed in Gaza, including nearly 16,500 children. More than 95,125 people have been wounded and more than 10,000 people are missing. Moreover, Israeli attacks have damaged or destroyed more than half of Gaza's homes, 80 percent of commercial facilities, 65 percent of road networks and 65 percent of cropland.[62] Seventeen of 36 hospitals are only partially functional.

---

61 https://www.theguardian.com/world/2024/jan/09/emissions-gaza-israel-hamas-war-climate-change

62 Data are from the United Nations Office for the Coordination of Humanitarian Affairs, the World Health Organization and the Palestinian government. See https://www.aljazeera.com/news/longform/2023/10/9/israel-hamas-war-in-maps-and-charts-live-tracker

And while the devastation in Gaza continues, settler and military violence is escalating in the occupied West Bank. On 28 August 2024, Israel launched its largest-scale military invasion of the occupied territory since 2002, targeting the Palestinian towns of Jenin, Tulkarm and Nablus and their camps. On the same day it was reported that the US had completed its 500th delivery of weapons to Israel since 7 October 2023. In Jenin, 'The occupying (Israeli) forces [had] demolished more than 70% of the city's streets completely ... to a depth of approximately one to one-and-a-half meters, which has led to the destruction of water and sewage networks, as well as communication and electricity cables.'[63]

In the West Bank, including East Jerusalem, at least 703 people have been killed, including more

---

63 https://www.middleeastmonitor.com/20240901-israel-destroyed-70-of-jenins-streets-infrastructure-says-municipality/

than 159 children, and more than 5,700 people have been injured.[64] Rosemary DiCarlo, Under-Secretary-General for Political and Peacebuilding Affairs cited the 'increasingly brazen and deadly' attacks carried out by Israeli settlers against Palestinians.[65] In early July 2024, Peace Now, a nonprofit organisation that monitors land confiscation in the West Bank, notes that Israel had seized 23.7sq km (9.15sq miles) of Palestinian land.[66] A report dated 20 August 2024 by the Commission of Detainees and Ex-Detainees Affairs stated that 10,200 Palestinians have been arrested in the West Bank and Jerusalem since 7 October 2023. This includes 350 women, 750 children and 94 journalists.[67]

---

64 https://www.aljazeera.com/news/longform/2023/10/9/israel-hamas-war-in-maps-and-charts-live-tracker

65 https://press.un.org/en/2024/sc15810.doc.htm

66 https://www.aljazeera.com/features/2024/7/19/how-israeli-settlements-are-taking-over-the-west-bank-as-gaza-war-rages

67 https://english.wafa.ps/Pages/Details/148259

On 2 September 2024, Benjamin Netanyahu appeared on television in front of a large map to present his plan for the future. There was no West Bank on that map.

GLOSSARY OF
ARABIC TERMS

Al-abjadiyah The Arabic alphabet, which consists
of 28 letters, all representing consonants. Text
is written from right to left in a cursive style.
The shape of each letter changes according to its
position in a word.

Batyeh A large, wooden bowl used to prepare dough
for bread, which is made from wheat flour, salt
and water.

Dabke A traditional Arab folklore line dance,
meaning 'to stomp the feet', which is often
performed at weddings and other celebrations.

Hummus A Levantine Arab thick paste made from
cooked ground chickpeas, tahini, lemon juice,
garlic and salt.

Keffiyeh A traditional Arab headdress worn by
Bedouins in historic Palestine. Though it comes
in a variety of colours, the black and white *keffiyeh*
was adopted by Palestinians in 1936 during the
Arab Revolt. It remains a symbol of Palestinian
solidarity and resistance. There are three main
patterns on the *keffiyeh* which have come to
symbolise important aspects of Palestinian life:
bold black stripes for the historical trade routes
that used to traverse Palestine; a fishnet pattern for

Palestinians' connection to the Mediterranean Sea; and a series of curvy lines for olive trees.

Labneh A soft Middle Eastern cheese made from strained yoghurt.

Marmoul A moulded Middle Eastern biscuit made of semolina flour and filled with dates.

Nada Dew.

Rababah The earliest known bowed instrument, with a single string, or two or three strings. It has a spike for resting on the ground, and is part of the lute (*oud*) family.

Saj A Middle Eastern unleavened flat bread traditionally cooked on a metal griddle.

Tabun A dome-shaped oven made of unbaked clay.

Tatreez Traditional Palestinian embroidery, most often used to decorate clothing. In 2021 *tatreez* was recognised by UNESCO as an intangible cultural heritage.

Thobe An ankle-length dress with long sleeves, adorned with hand-stitched embroidery.

Yallah habibti Let's go my love (feminine form). Habibi is the masculine form.

Za'atar A distinct herb in the mint family, similar to oregano and marjoram. *Za'atar* is known most widely, however, as a spice mix that is traditionally eaten with olive oil and bread or baked on top of dough. The ingredients of the spice mix vary from region to region but most often contain dried thyme, oregano, sumac and sesame seeds.

Zajjal A traditional oral strophic poet.

Zaytoun Olive.

Zir A large clay jug for storing water.

BIBLIOGRAPHY

Abdo, N. and Masalha, N. (eds) (2019), *An Oral History of the Palestinian Nakba*, Bloomsbury, London.

Abu Sitta, S. (2020), *The Atlas of Palestine, 1917–1966*, Palestine Land Society, London.

Allan, D. (ed.) (2021), *Voices of the Nakba: A Living History of Palestine*, Pluto Press, London.

Amiry, S. and Tamari, V. (2003), *The Palestinian Village Home*, Riwaq, Ramallah.

Ballad Films (2005), *I Remember 1948*, Documentary film, https://www.youtube.com/watch?v=N60GBVDBXrA

Blachnika-Ciacek, D. (2020), 'Occupied from Within: Embodied Memories of Occupation, Resistance and Survival among the Palestinian Diaspora', *Emotion, Space and Society,* Vol. 34, https://doi.org/10.1016/j.emospa.2019.100653

Brunner, B. (2012), *The Great Book Robbery*, Documentary film, https://www.youtube.com/watch?v=GdtCrCsKlw0&embeds_referring_euri=https%3A%2F%2Fbbrunner.eu%2F&source_ve_path=OTY3MTQ&feature=emb_imp_woyt

Chomsky, N. and Pappé, I. (2015), *On Palestine*, Penguin Books, London.

Goulordava, K. (2012), 'Scores of Palestinian Books, Nakba's Lesser Known Victims', *+972*

Magazine, 29 January, https://www.972mag.com/
documenting-scores-of-palestinian-books-nakbas-
lesser-known-victims/

Hallaj, M. (2008), 'Recollections of the Nakba
through a Teenager's Eyes', *Journal of Palestine
Studies*, Vol. 38, No. 1, https://www.palestine-
studies.org/en/node/42079#

Khalidi, W. (ed.) (1991), *All That Remains: The
Palestinian Villages Occupied and Depopulated by
Israel in 1948*, University of California Press,
Berkeley, CA.

Lughod, J.A. (1971), 'The Demographic
Transformation of Palestine', in Lughod, I.A.
(ed.), *The Transformation of Palestine*, Northwestern
University Press, Evanston.

Morris, B. (2011), *Righteous Victims: A History of
the Zionist–Arab Conflict, 1881–1998*, Knopf
Doubleday, New York.

Ong, A. (2023), '"My Village": Destroyed in
the Nakba, Rebuilt Memory by Memory',
https://www.aljazeera.com/features/
longform/2023/5/15/recreating-a-palestinian-
village-75-years-after-the-nakba

Pappe, I. (2007), *The Ethnic Cleansing of Palestine*,
Oneworld Publications, London.

Ziff, W.B. (2010 [1938]), *The Rape of Palestine*,
Martino Fine Books, Connecticut.

ACKNOWLEDGEMENTS

The Sunbird, like its central character, is slight, and it is filled with love and respect for the Palestinian people who have endured too much for too long. Despite its small size, many individuals enabled its publication.

I would like to thank the following people who read early versions of the manuscript and provided useful feedback and much-needed encouragement: Fiona Crawford, Tracy Goulding, Sonia Legge, Kate O'Grady and Marc Wilkins. And Cheryl Akle, Laura Benson, Lyn Harwood, Graeme Jones, Meg Keneally, Caitlin Reva and Sarkis Semaan for their willingness to help.

Thanks to Helen Benton who gave support from Aotearoa New Zealand; Letitia Davy who provided advice and guidance; and Steph Wilson who read the pages thoughtfully and with compassion.

I am thankful to Louis Haddad for his example, his stories and for verifying details of village life.

And to Salam Haddad who is no longer with us but fought hard and long.

Special thanks are due to the following people who gave their time and expertise: Rihab Charida, for positive feedback and advice on aspects Palestinian; Brigitta Doyle for so many things; Soren Goulding, editor and wise counsellor; Nikolai Haddad for his commitment to the cause and willingness to answer all my questions; Tam Morris for his exquisite artwork that perfectly captures the horror and the hope; and Karen Williams, tireless ally, who believes in this book as much as I do.

Francesca, thank you for your brave heart. And thank you Charles, for making everything possible.

Finally, I want to thank Amal Awad, Michelle de Kretser, Witi Ihimaera, Tom Keneally and Bruce Pascoe for making the time to read the story and for lending their names to it. And Aviva Tuffield at UQP for believing in *The Sunbird* and for taking it on its next journey.

DISCUSSION NOTES

1. The story of Nabila Yasmeen is prefaced by two quotes, the first from Mahmoud Darwish and the second from Winston Churchill. How did you feel reading each of these quotes? How do they frame Nabila's story?

2. *The Sunbird* is fiction based on oral and written histories. How does fiction help us to understand history? Conversely, how does the Addendum ground and frame the story?

3. Birds and birdsong appear as a motif throughout the story. What does this symbolise and how does it relate to the broader symbolism associated with Palestinian identity?

4. Consider the theme of 'uncertain futures' and discuss with examples of young Nabila's plans for her future and the older Nabila's habits and idiosyncrasies. What insights can we get from some of Nabila's rituals?

5. *The Sunbird* is told in time shift, taking the reader back and forth from the past into the present. What purpose do you think this serves and what effect did it have on your emotions while reading? What was similar and different between the two timeframes?

6. A yearning for home is a major theme in *The Sunbird*. What are some of the ways in which this is conveyed to the reader?

7. Discuss the symbolism, and the historical truth, of plants in this story. How do these work as metaphors for dispossession and colonisation?

8. What devices does the author use to emphasise the need to connect and belong to place?

9. Did you gain a different perspective on the experience of displacement after reading *The Sunbird*?

10. Can you compare the experience of dispossession described in *The Sunbird* to that of other people and places, and why?

11. Having read the book, if you had to explain the Nakba to a friend who knew nothing about it, how would you do this?

12. What purposes do peace rallies serve? Are they as much about a space to create solidarity and support as they are about sending a message to governments?

Thanks to Alissar Chidiac, Fiona Crawford, Jessica Frawley, Poppy Gee and Rochelle Pickles for their contributions to these questions.